Off We Go to Mexico!

An Adventure in the Sun

For my sister Ada, with love — L. K.
For Mike and Robert — C. C.

First published in Great Britain in 2006
by Barefoot Books, Ltd

Barefoot Books
124 Walcot Street
Bath BA1 5BG

This book has been printed on 100% acid-free paper

Graphic design by Louise Millar, London
Colour separation by Bright Arts, Singapore
Printed and bound by South China Printing Co. Ltd

This book was typeset in Hombre and Aunt Mildred
The illustrations were prepared in gouache on Fabriano paper

Hardback ISBN 1-905236-39-5

British Cataloguing-in-Publication Data:
a catalogue record for this book
is available from the British Library

1 3 5 7 9 8 6 4 2

Off We Go to Mexico!

An Adventure in the Sun

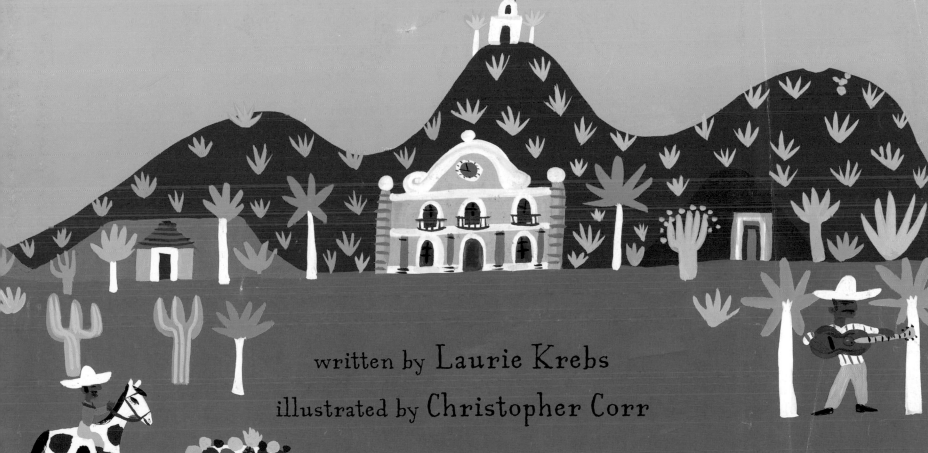

written by Laurie Krebs

illustrated by Christopher Corr

Barefoot Books
Celebrating Art and Story

OFF WE GO, OFF WE GO, OFF WE GO TO MEXICO!

water — **el agua**   beach — **la playa**

rocks — **las rocas**   whales — **las ballenas**

We swim in turquoise water and build castles on the beach.
We climb up rocks or watch from docks,
To see the grey whales breach.

train — **el tren**   bridge — **el puente**

mountains — **las montañas**   tunnels — **los túneles**

We hop aboard the canyon train. Across the bridge we go.
Up mountains steep, through tunnels deep,
We dare not look below.

festival — **la fiesta**   village square — **la plaza**

food — **la comida**   friends — **los amigos**

We hurry to a festival held in the village square.
There's food to eat and friends to meet
And laughter everywhere.

we climb — **subimos**   pyramids — **las pirámides**

now — **ahora**   long ago — **hace mucho tiempo**

We climb amazing pyramids from ancient Mexico
And wonder how they're standing now
When built so long ago.

music — **la música**   bands — **las bandas**
stars — **las estrellas**   we clap hands — **aplaudimos**

We tap our feet to music by the mariachi bands,
Who strum guitars beneath the stars
And sing, as we clap hands.

we trek — **caminamos**   villages — **los pueblos**

market — **el mercado**   things to buy — **las mercancías**

We trek to native villages, for this is market day.
Their rich supply of things to buy
Creates a bright display.

we hear — **oímos**   dancers — **las bailarinas**

costumes — **los vestidos**   beat — **el ritmo**

We circle round the plaza and we hear the stamping feet.
As dancers twirl, their costumes swirl
To the guitarists' beat.

butterflies — **las mariposas**   sunshine — **la luz del sol**

wings — **las alas**   sky — **el cielo**

We hike up to the winter home of monarch butterflies.
When sunshine brings a burst of wings,
Their glitter fills the skies.

flags — **las banderas** floats — **las carrozas**
flares — **los fuegos artificiales**
Independence Day — **Día de la Independencia**

We wave our flags, green, white and red. Parades are under way.
As floats pass by, flares fill the sky.
It's Independence Day!

capital — **la capital** park — **el parque**
zoo — **el zoológico** museums — **los museos**

We wander through the capital, where there's so much to see:
The park, the zoo, museums too,
And Aztec history.

ADIÓS, ADIÓS, ADIÓS TO MEXICO!

trip — **el viaje**   time — **la hora**

farewell — **adiós**   home — **la casa**

But now our trip is over and it's time to say farewell.
So home we go from Mexico —
We've got so much to tell!

CHIHUAHUAN
DESERT

SONORAN
DESERT

● COPPER
CANYON

Gulf of California

SIERRA MADRE OCCIDENTAL

■ La Paz

MEXICO

■ Guadalajara

Morelia ■

PACIFIC
OCEAN

UNITED STATES
OF AMERICA

Río Grande / Río Bravo

Gulf of Mexico

■ Monterrey

■ Guadalupe

SIERRA MADRE ORIENTAL

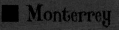

● TEOTIHUACÁN

■ Mexico
City

● PALENQUE

EL CHICHÓN ●

■ San Cristóbal
de las Casas

■ Oaxaca

SIERRA MADRE DEL SUR

RAINFOREST

BELIZE

GUATEMALA

HONDURAS

Mexico Today!

Some Facts about Mexico

Mexico is the eighth largest nation in the world and the third largest in Latin America after Brazil and Argentina. Mexico City is the capital. Nearly 20 million people live there, roughly a fifth of the total population.

The Rio Grande River (as it is known in the United States of America), or Río Bravo (its Mexican name), forms more than half of the northern border between Mexico and the USA.

The weather in Mexico is hot and humid along the coast and at sea level, but high in the mountains the temperature can drop below freezing. There are tropical rainforests in the south-east and desert areas in the north.

The Copper Canyon is a vast network of gorges, with at least four canyons that are deeper (at 1,800 metres/5,900 feet) than Arizona's Grand Canyon (at 1,425 metres/4,654 feet).

Every autumn, monarch butterflies travel south from the USA and Canada to spend the winter in the Sierra Madre mountains. In spring, the butterflies mate and lay their eggs before journeying back north.

Fiesta!

Mexicans love fiestas! Their calendar is filled with festivals. There's always lots of food, laughter and dancing, with traditional Mexican music played by strolling mariachi bands. Sometimes costumed folk dancers add to the celebration. Here are three of the most popular fiestas:

March or April — Semana Santa (Holy Week)

During Holy Week, Mexicans remember the last days in the life of Christ. Beginning on Palm Sunday with a jubilant parade, the week ends on Good Friday in a silent procession. Religious statues and a wooden cross are carried through the town. The Lenten fast is over and people await the joyous celebration of Easter.

Two Mondays in July — Guelaguetza (Mondays of the Hill)

High above the city of Oaxaca, a spectacular festival takes place. In ancient times, native people honoured the gods of rain and corn with a lively celebration of music and dance called the Guelaguetza. Today, troupes of skilful dancers, dressed in elaborate, colourful costumes, perform before the crowds.

15 and 16 September — Día de la Independencia (Independence Day)

This two-day holiday celebrates Mexico's independence from Spain. On the evening of 15 September, Mexico City's central plaza, or *zócalo*, is ablaze with lights and draped with banners of red, green and white. At midnight, the president repeats The Call to Freedom, first made in 1810 by Miguel Hidalgo, a parish priest. People cheer as the cathedral bells ring out and fireworks fill the sky.

The History of Mexico

The Ancient People (10,000 B.C.–A.D. 300)

Mexico's first people are believed to be hunter-gatherers who came from Russia and headed south. In time, they settled together in villages where they grew corn, beans and chilli peppers. They built huge pyramids and religious centres. One group, the Olmecs, carved great stone heads that looked part human and part animal.

The Classic Period (300–900)

The Zapotecs, living in the south, invented a written calendar and a form of writing called hieroglyphs, which uses pictures instead of words. In central Mexico, Teotihuacán was built — a magnificent city of temples and palaces. Around the same period, Maya culture spread throughout Mexico and beyond. Known for their spectacular pyramids, the Maya also improved the existing calendar and writing systems.

The Post-Classic Period (900–1521)

After the fall of Teotihuacán, the Toltecs, a northern tribe, moved into central Mexico. They were followed by the Aztecs. According to legend, the Aztecs built their city, Tenochtitlán, on the spot where an eagle, perched on a cactus, held a snake in its beak. Today, that place is the capital, Mexico City. Like the Toltecs before them, the Aztecs were great warriors. They believed that when they died in battle, they would turn into hummingbirds and fly to the sun, which they worshipped as their most important god.

The Conquest (1519-1524)

The Aztec empire was both rich and powerful when Hernán Cortés invaded Mexico. Sent by the Spanish king, Cortés arrived in 1519 and gained control of the Aztecs within two years, capturing their leader, Montezuma. In 1524, the Aztec nation fell completely.

The Colonial Period (1524-1821)

Under Spanish rule, most native Mexicans were very poor and often treated as slaves. Over time, their unhappiness grew and in 1810 the struggle for freedom began. Mexico finally became independent in 1821.

Independence (1821 to the present)

Independence did not come easily to Mexico. The country suffered several wars, acute poverty and many different leaders. Today there is hope for a peaceful future and a better life for everyone.

First Spanish Phrases

Hello	**Hola**
Goodbye	**Adiós**
See you later	**Hasta luego**
Pleased to meet you!	**¡Mucho gusto!/¡Encantado!**
Good morning	**Buenos días**
Good afternoon	**Buenas tardes**
Goodnight	**Buenas noches**
Thank you	**Gracias**
Please	**Por favor**
Yes/No	**Sí/No**
I don't understand	**No entiendo**
Please speak slowly	**Habla despacio, por favor**
How are you?	**¿Cómo estás?**
I'm fine, thank you	**Muy bien, gracias**
What is your name?	**¿Cómo te llamas?**
My name is . . .	**Me llamo . . .**
Where is . . . ?	**¿Dónde está . . . ?**
How do I get to . . . ?	**¿Cómo se llega a . . . ?**
How much does it cost?	**¿Cuánto cuesta?**

Barefoot Books
Celebrating Art and Story

At Barefoot Books, we celebrate art and story that opens
the hearts and minds of children from all walks of life, inspiring
them to read deeper, search further, and explore their own creative gifts.
Taking our inspiration from many different cultures, we focus on themes that
encourage independence of spirit, enthusiasm for learning, and sharing of
the world's diversity. Interactive, playful and beautiful, our products
combine the best of the present with the best of the past to
educate our children as the caretakers of tomorrow.

www.barefootbooks.com